THE ART OF
MANAGING
PEOPLE

A Simple Approach

Patrick M. Competelli

PUBLISH
AMERICA

PublishAmerica
Baltimore

Softcover 9781627721462
Hardcover 9781462661473
PUBLISHED BY PUBLISHAMERICA, LLLP
www.publishamerica.com
Baltimore

Printed in the United States of America

Dedication

This book is dedicated to my parents Lillian and Arthur Competelli for always being there for me. To my brother Tony, you were there when it counted bro, thanks. To my precious children Vincent and Alexa, you make every breath I take worth every minute of my life, and to my oldest son Michael for doing the right thing with your life.

PREFACE

This book was written from my personal arsenal of experiences. My point throughout this entire book is focused on treating your employees well, but within your means as a leader. Treat your employees exactly how you would like to be treated by your superiors. Too many people become supervisors and have the mindset that they must be heavy handed, or that they must dominate. This type of thought process tends to destroy morale and can create issues with production and customer service. You should help your employees to succeed in their careers by listening to their thoughts, educating them about your business, and by moving forward with some of their great ideas. The small percentage of employees that do not succeed despite your assistance, will weed themselves out through normal employee evaluation and disciplinary policies.

The best leaders will lead by example, as a leader get into the trenches with your employees. Good leaders show their employees that they have not forgotten where they came from. Leaders that slam their fist or lose control because of a power trip will burn out quickly and lose respect. Look back at the medieval times. The dictators that treated people with little regard were poisoned or killed in a violent manner. Leaders that rule by fear are perceived as not being very confident or competent and eventually people will fight back against the unfairness that they feel. The revolt will not happen in the beginning when a new leader begins his or her rein, it will happen in time. What keeps people from revolting in the beginning is the fear of losing their job. Employees will only speak among themselves for fear of repercussions from management. Leaders will not know what their employees are thinking until a union action takes place or a vote of no confidence is filed. Unfortunately, some leaders know exactly what they are doing to their employees, but they do not care. These types of leaders are driven by the power of the position. These leaders do not care to understand that respect from peers and employees is earned, you can never demand it; the word tyrant comes to mind with this type of leader.

This book is a simple approach to a management skill set that I learned during twenty-seven years of working in fire and emergency services. I learned by making mistakes and you will too. I hope that you get a lot out of reading this book, because I got a lot out of writing it.

Contents

CHAPTER 1:

THE UNHAPPY WORKPLACE

Throughout my history as an employee, I have enjoyed jobs, disliked jobs, and hated jobs. Sometimes I didn't like the work itself, for example when I was sixteen and worked down at the lake pulling weeds or when I was seventeen and worked at a gas station. There my boss had a smug attitude; he let you know that he was the boss. Each person will have his or her own story to tell.

I have seen managers, supervisors, and administrators make very poor decisions when it comes to employee morale. One issue that may ring true for some people is a situation where a less senior employee or an employee with less education or tenure is promoted to a leadership position. This situation can happen in any business. After one of these persons is promoted, they are sometimes tasked with supervising employees who have more understanding or experience with the product or service that the company provides. The tenured employees will most likely resent this individual. The less senior person who is promoted, may not know or understand what they are doing beyond the basics. Doesn't it make more sense to have someone who has already proven him or herself on the job to move up to a leadership position? These successful folks usually have customers and peers who respect them because of their knowledge, skills, and abilities. The tenured employee has most likely already made the mistakes that it takes to make you a better employee or an expert in your field. You may ask, what does making mistakes have to do with anything? Learning is the product of mistakes. Think about when you were a small child, you learned from your mistakes. If you touched a hot stove and are burned, you most likely will not touch the stove again. Usually after you break a few things or hurt yourself a few times, you know how to prevent those things from happening again; this is why experience is so important. The lessons you learn as an employee will enable you to be a better leader. You can help others not repeat your mistakes.

There are many employees who will have all the qualifications, education, respect and tenure necessary, but will still not get promoted. Why is that? It is unfortunate, but in the working world there are two terrible issues that stand out in my mind. One is called brown-nosing and the other is called the good-old-boy system. It is almost distasteful to broach these subjects; yet it is necessary. Is brown-nosing a way to be promoted? Can another employee who brown noses be a problem for other qualified individuals? My opinion is yes. The boss may promote someone who consistently works the angles, or as I mentioned, brown-nosed. This situation is bad for morale because the employees who are passed over for these specific reasons are the ones who are usually doing their jobs very well and are consistently doing other work that goes way beyond what is expected of them. The employee who is passed over will wince when the newly promoted "yes" person becomes their boss. It's a terrific letdown.

Let's discuss the mechanisms that make a promotion like this happen. Brown-nosers tend to look like they are working hard while the boss is around; they do whatever it takes to kiss up, then they slide backwards after the boss leaves. A brown-noser will do anything the boss asks them to do. This can even include spying on, and reporting fellow employees. If necessary, brown-nosers will sell their soul to the devil and send their own mother up the river to get a promotion. Brown-nosers will friend-up with the boss to the point of adopting their viewpoints and participating in the boss's favorite hobby. The brown-noser will latch on to whatever the boss is interested in, I have seen this first hand.

The good-old-boy system includes employees who have been friends with the boss for years. These employees are the incumbent simply based on the relationship itself. They are not family, that would be too obvious. They are friends who have worked with the boss for years. Relationships like this can get you a long way in corporate America. In many cases, a good-old-boy candidate will get the promotion. I believe that it is human nature to want someone that you know to be your sidekick. You know what they say, "It is sometimes who you know." This type of promotional process is the perfect formula to lower morale and production. When this type of promotional process goes on long enough, the employees who really deserve to be promoted, the ones that have worked for it, will start looking in the classifieds for a new job. What is even sadder about this situation is that the companies that allow these practices lose experienced people.

If you become a leader, don't get caught up in this sort of practice. Keep the morale of your employees where it should be, in the high range. High morale tends to yield high productivity. Try to see through the brown-nosers and do not hire or promote someone because of the good-old-boy system. I understand that this can be easier said than done. How can you not promote your kid brother's best friend? I understand the thought process behind these types of promotions, but all I can say is, you will have many personnel issues unless the person you promote is the most qualified person for the position.

Another big reason for having an unhappy workplace is based on how a leader treats his or her employees. Promotions are one thing, but your workplace environment will make a difference as well. An extremely important approach to keeping your employees happy and productive is that you remain openly fair and consistent. Being unfair, or the perception of unfairness in the areas of promotion or discipline, will cost the company. Employees may steal, mount work slowdowns, build inferior products, or do other things to hurt a corporation. A reduction in sales is something you do not want. As a leader you are looking for a happy, prideful, and enthusiastic workforce that will produce and score your company top dollar sales. You also want your employees to provide excellent service to your customers. If you do not want any of this for your company, simply disregard everything you have just read.

You may have noticed that I have not yet discussed wages and benefits. The reason for this is that wages and benefits are typically short lived morale boosters. It is great to receive more money in your paycheck, and it would be fantastic to have the best benefits in the world, but most people will not dwell on these issues when deciding if they are happy in their workplace or not. If you have an employee who has an outstanding workplace environment with little to no stress, and a boss who cares about them, the wages and benefits seem to take a back seat. This might be hard to grasp but it is true. Of course the ideal situation is a balance of pay and benefits. This is why unions were born. Nobody should have to work in a sweatshop for minimum wage and terrible or even no benefits. If you have a job with the total package meaning, a great management team with outstanding benefits and wages, that's awesome.

This chapter only discusses a few examples of what may cause an unhappy workplace. As you read the next several chapters, all the issues discussed in this chapter will hopefully tie together for you. In the meantime, see what happens if you change your management style to one that provides more care to your employees; I think you will be surprised with what happens.

CHAPTER 2:

FAVORITISM ON THE JOB

Favoritism on the job is another one of those things that will likely cause an issue. If you allow an employee to be late to work, or you allow a certain employee or a group of employees to be assigned to the shift they want, this will be viewed as favoritism. Maybe you allow someone to get off work at the last minute, but you will not allow others to do the same thing. When employees are not treated the same way, it tends to create a rivalry. Employee bickering and even physical violence may result; we can do without either of these at the workplace. Favoritism leads directly to disrespect for organizational leadership. Just the perception of favoritism is another issue that an employee will not speak about publically. Do not poop in your own back yard so to speak, it may be considered a road to career suicide. So what do employees who feel there is favoritism do? They frown and bear it, at least for a little while. You should be prepared for the possibility of legal ramifications from the employees who feel they are being affected.

Throughout my career I have witnessed favoritism directly. Each time I was personally passed over for a promotion, I felt emotionally drained. It took me over twenty years to realize that unfortunately it can be who you know. I have seen this happen repeatedly to some good people, not just myself. Many of you reading this book know what I am talking about and although I understand why it happens, it does not make it right. Some leaders who play favorites do not care about the legal ramifications or they simply do not know any better; I have seen both. I have also seen this issue destroy morale, and destroy a cohesive working environment. I talk about favoritism again in the chapter on promotions because favoritism can and does play a huge role there as well.

An example of favoritism that happened to me at "Any Fire Department USA" was when there was an opening for a Training Chief position. We needed one of the current District Fire Chiefs to fill the position until we could promote someone. I was the only District Fire Chief who volunteered to cover the slot, but to everyone and my surprise, and right in front of me the

Fire Chief asked someone else to do it. There were six of us in the room and we all looked at each other. The person the Fire Chief asked to cover the slot said, "Chief, Pat said he would do it." The Fire Chief was still not happy and asked again for this other District Chief to cover the slot.

Another Chief in the room, in a disgusted tone said, "Chief, Pat said he will fill the slot, he said he will do it." By the end of the meeting, I was set to fill the slot for the next six months. The other District Fire Chief who the Fire Chief wanted, did not have more training or certifications than I did, the Fire Chief simply liked him better and he made that known. The meeting and what took place at the meeting made me feel like crap and made everyone else feel very uncomfortable. Do not do this to an employee, especially in front of his or her peers. I tell you my "Any Fire Department USA" stories so that you have real situations to reference and to learn from, not because I am whining. These situations unfortunately are not out of the norm for some professional organizations.

I want to discuss the situation of you as a leader having a friendship with a subordinate; how can this situation be perceived as favoritism? It is perfectly acceptable to be friends with your employees, but do not let your friendship become something that looks like favoritism. For example, if you have a fishing buddy that you have known for years and you are promoted to this person's direct supervisor, does this mean you can't go fishing with them anymore? No, it does not; however, it does mean that you need to be aware of your relationship being viewed as a favoritism issue. You can do everything in your power to be fair, but when you are seen spending time and socializing with him during work the bottom line is, people think you are treating him or her differently. This is a perception, and you may not be able to change that. Keep in mind that as hard as it is, you must consider the ramifications of other employees gossiping about almost anything you do that appears like you are favoring a friend. Perception is hard to overcome. Perception translates to fact to many people. Make it very clear to all, and I do not mean verbally; actions speak much louder then words. Make it very clear by your actions, that no matter who the people are, everyone will be treated exactly the same, including friends. Let all employees see that you are treating your pal the same as everyone else. The hard part about this whole situation is realizing that you may lose a friendship over this. Sometimes even friends will put us into a situation that could cause us to lose our job, or to lose respect from other employees. If your friend does not understand the fine line between work and friendship, you may need to re-evaluate your relationship.

A simple fact is that everyone wants to make sure that they get as much as everyone else. This also translates to each person wanting to be treated with the same respect that a leader or manager gives to everyone else. Here is a real life example of what I mean.

During my tenure as a leader, I have had to discipline some of my friends. I have even had to fire a couple of them. It is not a comfortable thing to do, but you have to go by the rules and regulations no matter who the employee is. Make sure that all the reasons for discipline or termination are correct. The key is to make sure that you do not skirt any issues, or make things easier on any one individual. Sometimes this is hard to do and frankly, people commit this type of mistake all the time. If this were not an issue in the workplace, I would not be writing about it. I can assure you however, if you act in a prejudiced manner long enough, it will eventually be the end of your career as a leader.

The Reader's Digest version is this, if you are a police officer, make sure you are willing to give your mother a speeding ticket. Weigh all of your options and if you do not issue the ticket, make sure that you treat everyone else that has the same infraction the same way. Help your employees to understand that you are required to be legally and ethically fair and consistent to everyone no matter who they are, or who they know. Good employees will respect this fact and they will not put you in a situation that could cause you a problem with your superiors.

My advice is simple. Never favor any one employee or group of employees. Think before you act. How will your actions make an employee or employees feel? Try not to shoot from the hip. Remember favoritism or the perception of favoritism is an issue that you do not want at your workplace.

CHAPTER 3:

DISCIPLINE

Discipline is a broad topic. There are employees that will respond to general supervision without the need for discipline and there are those, usually in the minority, that will attempt to play the system. Most employees have an understanding of the basic principles of right and wrong. The basic premise is, 'if I break the rules, I am going to get in trouble.' No matter what type of business you are in, the majority of the employees will follow the rules. With the small percentage of employees that do not follow the rules, you will need to move in one of three directions. Coaching and counseling, progressive discipline, or immediate termination. I will explain each one of these options.

Coaching and counseling is a notification to the employee letting them know that they broke a rule, or that they may have come real close to stepping over the line of breaking a rule. Coaching and counseling is more of a tap on the shoulder and a reminder to the employee to be careful. With coaching and counseling formal discipline is not issued, but you create a file and place the documentation in that file for future use. If there is another occurrence of the same issue, you will have documentation to use in further dealings with the employee. To be clear, coaching and counseling leads directly to progressive discipline. This is my preferred method of entering the disciplinary arena, it is more like educating an employee before entering into a more formal disciplinary process. When I first started using it some of my colleagues were less than thrilled. I was ridiculed and told that I was not hard enough on my employees, that my employees would just continue doing the wrong things and that they would walk all over me. I found that this was not the case at all. I found that I received a lot of respect because they knew that they could be human and make some mistakes. Some supervisors think that coaching and counseling is just a free ride. But as I said earlier, the employee that does not respond to coaching and counseling will enter a more formal disciplinary process.

Before you can begin any type of disciplinary process, this includes coaching and counseling; you must set up clear and concise ground rules for everyone. If the current employees do not understand the guidelines, the newer employees most certainly will not either. If you are just taking over a department, or even if you have been there for a while, make sure that the rules and regulations are clear and easy to read. Along with the rules and regulations, you must have a list of the consequences, a disciplinary policy. It should be very clear what the punishment is for each infraction.

Progressive discipline is the most widely used form of discipline at the workplace; it is like a three strikes and you are out approach. Progressive discipline allows you to advise the employee that they broke a rule, and it allows the employee time for training to avoid repetition of the digression. This process is more formal.

Since this version of my book is basic, I will not go any further on how to set up a disciplinary process itself. What I want to do instead, is to walk you through a real progressive disciplinary issue that I was part of; I believe that many of your questions may be answered by this example. I had an employee who worked with me at "Any Ambulance Service USA." This employee was one of the best Emergency Medical Technicians (EMTs) that I had ever worked with. Robert had just one problem, he showed up late to work. We all know that no matter where you work if you are not on time for the job, it is a huge issue. Here is how I handled Robert's tardiness from start to finish. The name "Robert" and all the dates and times are fictitious, but the discipline and what I describe taking place is real.

On the first day Robert was late, I did not receive a call from him stating that he was going to be late for work. We all know that things happen, that is why we have sick leave and other types of leave on the books, so if you are going to be late or miss work, you should call. Robert showed up five minutes after the start of his work shift as verified by the time clock at the "Operations Supervisor's Office." I see Robert scanning his card and I say, "Hi Robert, what's up?"

Robert turns with a red face and says, "I know, I know, I am sorry, it will never happen again." I asked Robert to step into my office. I did not make a huge deal about it because there were other employees around. I asked Robert why he was late. Robert advised me that he had left his house later than usual. According to the current disciplinary manual, I could have tagged Robert with a verbal warning. This would have been strike one. What I decided to do is speak to Robert about lateness and explain how being late for his shift again could cause him to receive discipline. I really felt that Robert understood what I had to say, so I administered a coaching and counseling form. Remember that coaching and counseling is a buffer for a first offense when it is used. Robert was thankful for my leniency and he went to work. So what happened the following week? Yep, Robert strolled in five minutes late; here is how that situation played out. I asked Robert to step into my office and I closed the door behind him. Just closing the door is a psychological clue to the employee that something is not good. I asked Robert to have a seat, and I said, "You know what happens now right?"

Robert said, "Discipline?"

I said, "Yes. I wish that we didn't have to do discipline but you brought the situation on yourself."

Robert nodded in the affirmative. I asked him, "What happened? I'm surprised that you're late again especially since I let you slide the previous week."

Robert had no real answer, he just apologized. I pulled the disciplinary manual from my desk drawer; it was very quiet in the office as I looked up the section on being late to work. After I found the section on tardiness and I opened to that page, I turned the book around and showed Robert why he was going to receive discipline. He and I also discussed what happens if he is late again. The first formal discipline that Robert received was called a verbal warning for being late. Although the discipline is called a verbal warning, there is documentation of the occurrence and the documentation clearly states "Verbal Warning" at the top. All the information for the discipline is neatly placed on the computer-generated form. The form contains all the essential information and a place for the employee and the supervisor to comment and to sign. This was an easy one because the investigation was right in front of me. I had seen the employee report late to work two times. Other situations could take months of investigation prior to coming up with the most appropriate discipline.

On this particular case, I went over all the paperwork with Robert and I asked him if he would like to comment verbally or in writing about the discipline. He declined both. At this point, he and I signed the form. This next part is very important. After I issued the verbal warning, I made it very clear that the next time Robert is late, he would receive a written warning for being tardy. I also told him that the next step after that is a written warning of termination. The last discipline to be issued after the termination warning is termination. I made sure that Robert understood how things were going to work from here forward; he indicated that he did. At this point, I sent Robert to work and I filed the paperwork in the employee's personnel file. That was that, so I thought. I will cut to the chase. Robert no longer works for "Anytime Ambulance Service USA." He finally made it all the way through the process and got himself fired.

The meeting went kind of like this. Robert showed up to work and I asked him to step in the supervisor's office. He had a worried look on his face, so I did not keep him waiting. I explained to Robert that he was terminated and I went over his personnel file with him. Robert did not put up any kind of a fight, he said ok and he left quietly. I told him that we would be in touch about getting all of his equipment. Terminating someone is not an easy thing to do, especially if you know the person well, but if it has to be done, it has to be done.

Immediate termination is the harshest choice in a disciplinary process and it is rarely used. An employee must do something to the extreme in order for management to terminate. Some examples of these types of infractions would be to get caught stealing, hurting another employee, or attempting to cause the company to lose money in a malicious manner. In these cases, you have just cause to terminate the employee. With these issues on the table, you must have all your ducks in a row, and you must have all the pertinent evidence and necessary documentation. Out of all the disciplinary actions that I discuss, immediate termination is the one that will land you in court. This is because an employee would be more likely to attempt to sue your company for what they consider wrongful termination. Even if you followed all the rules and regulations and filed all the proper paperwork, some people will still attempt to sue your company out of rage or because they feel that they were somehow treated unfairly. You need to be very prepared in all cases of discipline, and as I said earlier, do not shoot from the hip.

Other issues when it comes to discipline depend on who you work for. I have personally worked for supervisors who did not give you the slightest bit of a break. In other words, if you broke something, or missed dotting an "I" or crossing a "T", they disciplined you, no questions asked. In the discipline realm of employment, you must be careful about how much discipline you hand out. Discipline can greatly affect employee morale. I am not saying that you should not discipline someone who actually deserves it. I am saying to separate the deliberate breaking of a rule from the accidental situation that can be fixed with training or coaching and counseling. As I stated previously if you discipline people for all of their humanistic errors and mistakes, you leave no room for the employees to learn. You must allow your employees time to learn from their mistakes without having fear of punishment. If you do not follow this simple advice, you will have many employees walking around afraid to touch the equipment that they work with. The employees will be stressed and worried that if they are not perfect the hammer will drop. Unfortunately, too many companies allow their leaders or supervision teams to operate in this manner; let me explain what this does.

This type of management style can take your best employees and make them basket cases. These employees dread coming to work and they try to stay well below the radar screen. Employees who feel this way tend to be jumpy and walk the other way when they see you coming. Do not create this type of working environment.

I want to go over some examples of why an employee may make mistakes that would require discipline. As I explained earlier in this chapter, most discipline can be avoided by supplying proper training. If after a multitude of training attempts the employee continues to falter, you may need to start the progressive disciplinary process to remove the employee from service. With that said, I believe that most employees are salvageable. Keeping good employees comes down to leadership. I explain different leadership styles later in this book, but I need to mention here that employees who feel they are being continuously watched or targeted by their supervisor have a tendency to suffer undue stress. This also retards them from being creative and to let their imaginations soar with things that would be helpful to the company. Take the employee that has been around for a long time and has an excellent record. This employee is suddenly acting up and making mistakes, or this employee reams out another employee. As a manager, you should not be drooling to discipline that employee. You should be responsible and find out what is going on with this employee. Why is the employee acting this way? I can tell you that a job in law enforcement and fire or emergency medical services, causes plenty of hard core stress. These employees are under intense emotional stress throughout their day. One day I received discipline from a supervisor who loved to discipline people;

let me explain. A situation happened with a co-worker where we had a disagreement about the hospital destination for a trauma patient. A little background. I had ten years seniority over this particular co-worker and I worked part-time for the Medical Director, this is the doctor who makes these particular decisions for all the paramedics in the EMS (emergency medical services) system. So to say the least, I was a little upset that there was a disagreement about my recommendation. In the end, the Medical Director was called on the radio and he backed up my decision. I went home after my shift and stewed for a while about what happened. I ultimately made a terrible decision about how to handle my frustration. I confronted my co-worker a few days later; I did not curse or say anything awful; the confrontation was not physical. I just explained my unhappiness with the way things went on the emergency call. I said that I could not believe there was a disagreement, especially since the co-worker knew of my background and experience in this area. Well, word got back to my supervisor and I was disciplined severely for the confrontation. The supervisor I had at the time was the kind of individual who really got off on filling out the paperwork. I am not mentioning this in my book because I am bitter. I am mentioning this because this type of management style can destroy your career as a leader and can hurt the career of your employee. I am recalling this story and putting myself out there to teach a lesson. To this day, no one has sat the two of us employees down to fix the problem. There was no attempt to find out why I was so upset in the first place. In the end, I took it upon myself to patch things up with my co-worker and our friendship was mended. It was obvious that the manager who handed out the discipline cared about the discipline more than a good and fair result. This is an outstanding example of how not to use the disciplinary process. As I stated earlier when you have a situation like this one you need to find out why. Is it stress? Is it the lack of training? Is it dependency on illegal substances? What caused the situation with another employee? You need to do your homework and figure out what happened.

My recommendation on how to handle most employee disciplinary issues is this. First, you need to review the problem from A-Z. Do not leave any stone unturned because that will catch up with you. Trust me, the cunning employee who is getting discipline will have all his or her cards ready to go. Second, make sure that you have all the required documentation in place. Your company may require incident reports or verbal testimony. After you gather all the facts from everyone involved, (and what ever you do, do not leave out a single person who is said to be, or is directly involved), ask yourself if this is a situation where you need to go to the employee and find out if they are having problems due to stress. Or is it something else. Some examples of stressors could be did Mom or Dad die? Was someone close to the employee diagnosed with cancer? Whatever it is, just asking the employee will show that you are thinking about their well-being. After a full investigation and fact-finding mission, determine what you have found. If the employee is truly at fault, lay out all the facts for the employee and explain the rules and regulations that they have violated. At this point, give the employee a chance to explain why they may agree or disagree with your findings. If you find that the employee has reasons for disagreeing with you, determine if they have new information that could change the outcome of your investigation. If you find that new information does not in any way require you to conduct further investigation and in no way changes your findings, it is at this point that you will apply the discipline. If you find that you need to do further research to back up the employee's new story or evidence, you should take the time to conduct further research. After you apply discipline, explain to the employee that this mistake is recoverable. Have a short training session explaining to the employee how he or she can stay out of this kind of trouble in the future. Never act as if you are enjoying giving the employee the discipline; rather that you have no other choice based on the employee's infraction. Show the person the printed text in the sections of the rules and regulations that they violated, this is so they can realize that you are just doing your job.

Usually an employee will not repeat the same offense twice. An employee will learn that what they did is unacceptable and that the consequences of a repeat offense will not be favorable. If an employee does commit the same infraction a second time, immediate action to include heavier discipline will occur. A third offense should constitute either dismissal or a final written warning of termination. If you do keep an employee with multiple infractions, you may want to enter into a last chance agreement or 'memorandum of understanding' (MOU). The (MOU) should state the reason for its implementation and should spell out exactly what will happen if a similar event occurs again. The usual consequence of having another issue while already in an (MOU) is immediate termination. You should check with your Human Resources Department and make sure that you can even offer such an instrument as an (MOU).

Another direction you can go before you apply discipline is to get the troubled employee help from a counselor, clergy, or a friend. If an employee falls under your immediate termination policy for the things they have done, but you feel they have a mental issue, you can send the employee to an employee assistance program (EAP) instead of terminating the employee. If you choose to go down this path because you feel that the employee has a problem that will not respond to regular coaching and counseling techniques, discuss this option with the employee and your Human Resources Department. It would not be fair to terminate or discipline this type of special needs employee without first attempting another route. People, especially in fire and emergency medical services, the military, and the police department can suffer from Post-Traumatic Stress Disorder (PTSD). This disorder can result in odd and sometimes irrational behavior. Although this book will not cover mental health issues, nor am I qualified to discuss or teach them, I encourage all managers and supervisors who deal with these high-risk employees to obtain some training in this area.

To conclude this chapter on discipline, infractions of rules can range from calling out sick to injuring another employee, theft, and incompetence. You have to apply discipline techniques to your own company's playing field. In some instances, there will be an occurrence that may require immediate termination. Make sure you review all cases thoroughly and that you have all the necessary information in order to follow through with any type of discipline. You should always review the employee's prior work history before making a disciplinary decision. Has there been other occurrences of the same type? Decide what type of discipline will fit the occurrence; coaching and counseling, progressive discipline, or immediate termination as written in your company's disciplinary guidelines. Check to see if you can use a memorandum of understanding (MOU), in your disciplinary process and remember; you should want your employees to succeed. Do not set your employees up for failure because of your need for power. You should have the attitude that you would rather the employee produce a good product or deliver a good service. You should hope that the disciplinary policy book is on a shelf with the pages turning yellow, this is a better alternative than having to discipline or terminate your employees. Help your employees learn how to stay out of trouble; it can be a win, win situation.

CHAPTER 4:

PROMOTIONS

My advice on promotions is that you do not promote someone just because they happen to be your favorite employee, or based on race or gender. Promote someone because of his or her qualifications. Promoting someone who is under qualified, or that is not the absolute best applicant for the job, regardless of race, sex, age, religious or political beliefs, is simply not the right thing to do. When it comes to promotion, you should review a person's résumé, tenure, education, employee record and experience. You should bring all these pieces together, conduct an interview, and then make an informed and educated decision. The best person for the position will be a person that is very well rounded and who meets all of the qualifications for the position. Usually a position is posted on the bulletin board and the job will list several required qualifications. The qualifications list may request that the applicant have a degree, a certain amount of time on the job and a few other relevant certifications. Sometimes at the very end of the qualifications list there might be a line that says, if you do not have all of the required qualifications, "you can have an equivalent combination of education, training and experience that provides the required knowledge, skills and abilities." Now this is only my opinion, but this last line possibly leaves the position open to less qualified applicants. I also perceive this verbiage as giving the authorities involved in the process, free rein to hire their buddy. The "combination of" statement can be interpreted many different ways. Again, this is only my opinion. If you leave the paperwork as needing a degree, fewer people will most likely be eligible for the position. In requiring a degree, you will gather people that not only meet time parameters and other important requirements, they also have an education to go along with that experience. I do not want you to think that every time you see the "combination of" statement that someone is pulling a fast one, I just want you to keep in mind that this practice does change the playing field.

It is unfortunate, but politics can play heavy over qualifications in the workplace.

As a manager, make sure you list the qualifications you are truly looking for, stand by them when you move forward with your testing and hiring process. Make the qualification paperwork straight forward and to the point. If you are going to hire someone who does not have a degree or the necessary management experiences as listed in the requirements, do not bother putting those requirements on the qualifications list. It will be obvious when the person you hire does not fit the qualifications. Remember what I keep saying in other chapters, "remain fair and consistent."

It all depends what you want to do when you promote. Do you want the employee to meet the minimal requirements for the job, or are you looking for someone with a little more education and experience? I personally recommend that you look more towards a person with at least some education, unless it is not needed for a particular position. With that said, I know from firsthand experience that not all persons with degrees or a higher education can put the bookwork they acquired towards the technical stuff. For example, an educated person may not be able to bring the knowledge to the sales floor, or an educated medical professional may not be able to bring their knowledge to the accident scene. Sometimes the learned information cannot make it from the head to the hands. This is why a testing component with both written and skills testing may be necessary. In the Fire service, we test for just about all of our promotional positions. As luck and hard work would have it, I ranked number one on the District Fire Chief promotional exam, so I am finishing this book as a District Fire Chief instead of a Lieutenant. This advancement allows me to help make this point. I was able to apply for the position of District Fire Chief based on a years on the job requirement. I was then promoted because I scored number one on the exam; nothing else really mattered. My degrees and my work record had no bearing on my getting the position. At the time of the promotion, I held a Bachelor's degree. I can apply that knowledge to the day-to-day job that I will do, but as I said, my having a degree was only by chance. Another candidate could have obtained a higher score on the test and have received the promotion without a formal education. As I said prior, education is not the end all be all, but I do believe it is relevant for both an employer and employee. Testing results can be very helpful in a promotional process. Testing may, or may not tell you that the person is the absolute best candidate, but it is a very good tool in leveling out the playing field. When you conduct testing, I recommend that you use an independent outside testing agency. By using an independent testing agency from outside of your workplace, there is less chance or perception that a candidate was picked over others due to favoritism.

Here is another example of what happened to me at the "Any Fire Department USA." In promotional opportunities above District Fire Chief, testing was not required. You simply had to meet the requirements for the interview process, which was for example, five or more years in a chief position. As in other promotional processes, the posting for this job that I was going for requested a degree or, blah, blah, blah, that meets the knowledge skills and abilities for the position. Once the Human Resources Department determined that you met the qualifications, you would be scheduled for an interview. The interview is scored in a subjective manner and the candidate who scores highest is picked. I will tell you straight out, I was the best candidate for three positions. I was passed over each time because the Fire Chief wanted someone else. What made this very sad and caused internal morale issues, is that people from outside our agency filled two of the three positions. Most of the firefighters that I worked with were beside themselves. I had twelve years with the Department, I had a

Masters Degree, I was already a District Fire Chief, and this was the next position in the chain of command; the "Operations Chief." I had trained for this position, and I had proven my command and leadership skills. My boss did not want me in the position and that is why I did not get it. You may want to say that I am just whining, but this situation is true. I wound up leaving the department to take a job as a Fire Chief elsewhere. Out of over three hundred candidates for the other Fire Department, I was hired. This did not go unnoticed by my peers from the department that I had just left.

Let us discuss employee tenure. What does employee tenure tell you? It tells you that the employee has given some thought to remaining at your company or workplace, especially if they are applying for a promotion. Some employees will remain on a job for years and never apply for a promotion because they are happy at the bottom. I knew of several firefighters who stayed firefighters for over twenty-five years and never wanted to be promoted; I say good for them. So why count experience? This is for the obvious reason. People who have been around for a while and that have been excelling in their jobs, are naturally the ones who you would want to appoint to lead and teach others. Use the employee's experience and previous job performances as you or the employee's direct supervisors· have witnessed. Allow this information to help you in your decision making process. Many people wish to be promoted, but if they do not have some experience in doing the job they want to lead, how can they work the position as a supervisor. This is another double-edged sword. I for instance cannot be a train conductor supervisor; I have never held that job before, so how can I supervise it? On the other hand, I have been in fire and emergency services for over twenty-five years, so I am fit for most positions in that arena. I believe that employee tenure means something, and you should consider giving points for tenure.

Next, let us look at the employee record, this can tell you a lot. Has the employee received good evaluations? Did they commit offenses regarding rules and regulations on a consistent basis? Have the rules they broke been serious or simple? This analysis should weigh into the mix, but only to a point. As I stated earlier people have to make mistakes in order to learn. I think that you need to review the record, and if the employee has had some issues that have not arose in years, they should not count against them in the promotional process. You may want to consider using a time window for issues that deal with the employee's disciplinary record. In other words, if the employee has something that is five years old, it simply does not count. Here is a curve ball for you. If you want the employee record to count 100% for everyone, then you need to create a rating process for each infraction that you will count against every employee the same way. Another problem here is if someone is playing favorites and wants to disregard someone for promotion, the employee record could be the route used to discriminate. Please remember that I am not a lawyer; I am just offering you food for thought.

What about when there are opportunities for advancement in your company, but you have never had the opportunity to work in that particular position? I hear this all the time from people. "How can I get the experience if I am never assigned or trained to do that particular job?" For example, you are an electrician and there is only one position to be promoted into, the assistant head electrician position. You have been an electrician for thirteen years but you never had much opportunity to train in the assistant head electrician position which deals with management type decision making. The authorities may tell you that you do not have the necessary management experience to apply for that position. This is very discouraging to many employees. This is why I believe very strongly in creating mentoring programs to eliminate these issues. With a mentoring program, you give your employees an opportunity to receive training in one or even more positions within the company. A mentoring program gives an employee the necessary experience that they will need if the situation arises for them to move up. If your mentoring program allows shadowing an immediate supervisor, the employee can learn exactly how to do that job, and the employees in the program will be all set when the time comes for a promotion to that position.

Lastly, we will discuss the employee résumé. The résumé is more important to review for an employee that you are hiring from outside of the company, someone that you have no history with, a person that you really know nothing about. A résumé can say a lot about a person. Is the résumé on nice paper? Is it well written? You should not base the whole enchilada on the résumé, but you should review the résumé for content. You should make sure that the information can be verified, and you should match up the person's qualifications with your requirements for the position.

I had to review résumés for an open position that I was on the hiring board for. Several things that stood out on the résumé for me was the paper, the cleanliness, and the presentation. I felt very good about a résumé that was on a heavier stock paper. I also liked the résumé that was not overly stuffed with what I call fluff. Fluff is an accumulation of information that the applicant puts on the résumé because they want you to think that they have more experience than·they really have. This is all in contrast to a résumé that I had seen that was printed on very cheap paper, with coffee stains, and that was held together with a paperclip that kept falling off.

The bottom line when it comes to promotions is to use the resources that are available to you so you promote the right person for the job. Make sure that you write the requirements solely based on what you are actually looking for in a candidate. If you are going to test, make sure that the testing is fair. Make sure that you penalize all applicants the same way if you are going to take off points for things in the employee discipline record. Make your decision based on sound judgment. Do not appear as if you are playing favorites, or that you are deliberately keeping someone out of the promotional process; it is obvious when this happens. Take yourself out of the equation if possible and as I stated earlier when I discussed testing, hire an independent outside agency to conduct your promotional processes. If you hire an independent company that is reputable and you keep your hands off of the entire processes, you will most likely have no issues with the promotions that take place and your employees will appreciate the fairness of the process.

CHAPTER 5:

SUPERVISOR TYPES

"The big chip supervisor"

When I first became a supervisor some fifteen years ago, I was a complete jerk. I yelled at people who did not follow directions, and I embarrassed people in front of their peers. I really did not know how to harness the big chip I had on my shoulder. When I received all that power, I went wild with it. It took me about three months to realize that people do not respond well to that type of supervisor; people want to be respected. Because of my personal experience, the first supervisor type I want to discuss is the one that I originally was, "the big chip supervisor." The big chip supervisor makes every situation a major one. The first thing I realized is as a big chip supervisor, I was being alienated; no one wanted to be around me. When I walked up to a crowd, people stopped talking and nervously said, "Hello." They only said hello out of necessity because I was the boss, not because they had any respect for me. It was more for the six gold stripes that I wore on my shoulders. People hid things from me and they did not want me around. I felt the employee resentment on a daily basis, and guess what? My job was not fun anymore. I completed my missions night after night. I took the call outs, I filled the shifts, and I did the payroll. However, I lacked a feeling of enjoyment from being a supervisor and being a supervisor was all I wanted to do. I sat down with myself and I realized that I was young. I was about twenty-five when I was promoted. I had no real formal experience in management, so I learned about leadership the hard way, by making mistakes. Even though I succeeded in getting the company's needs accomplished, the money side of the business, I was lacking greatly in caring for my employees. I supervised approximately one-hundred personnel at any given time of the day or night. I was the supervisor for a countywide private ambulance company. I worked the five at night to five in the morning shift. Like I said, I got the job done, but I wanted to be a more effective supervisor, so this is what I did. I started carrying a cooler of soda in my vehicle. Every time I met up with a crew, I offered them a soda;

sort of a peace offering. I stayed with the crew at their ambulance post, and I talked to the crew as if they were the most important thing to me at that very moment. I asked the crew how the shift was going, I asked them if they needed anything. No one really wanted much, but at least I asked. When I left the ambulance post I told the crew to have a good night and if they needed anything to call me. This was a good start towards a change for me, and I heard positive things about my visits through the grape vine.

Another thing I started to do dealt with employee errors. When an employee did make a mistake, I took them in the office and spoke to them in a normal tone. I never raised my voice and I made sure that they knew that I would do a full investigation based on all the facts. The employee knew that I would only follow through with discipline if necessary. If I could get through to the employee by coaching and counseling, or by providing re-education or training, that is what I would do. I felt that this was enough punishment, especially if the employee walked in telling me that they screwed up. You need to be aware of the empathetic employee that may take advantage of your good nature in order to get off easy. If you find out that you were fooled into letting someone slide, you know what to do the next go around. You know not to trust that employee and you change your strategy when dealing with that employee. Remember that old phrase, "once bitten, twice shy". People started to see that I cared about them. My employees responded to this method of leadership in a positive manner. People started to hope that I was on duty. They came to me with their problems, both personal and job-related. I had gained their respect and they trusted me. They knew that I wouldn't let them slide to far off course because I had a job to do, but they knew if they got into trouble, I would be fair and consistent every time. I found that my employees started doing their best to keep me from having to be a supervisor, they wanted to do their jobs to the best of their abilities. I had become a well-balanced supervisor.

"The well balanced supervisor"

The well-balanced supervisor consists of little bits and pieces of each supervisory style all rolled into one nice package. This person can handle just about any company or employee need. The well-balanced supervisor can adapt to any situation and they can apply different management styles based on different employee types. This type of leader is viewed in a professional and respected manner. The well-balanced supervisor has an aura of confidence that everyone seems to feed off of. This supervisor has merits that stand on their own and their management style is not offensive to anyone; their accomplishments in the workplace are usually outstanding. We all know that amongst people are different personality types. Some people are harsh, some are kind, and some people are just way out there and hard to understand at all. The well-balanced supervisor can figure out an employee's personality type and apply a management style that best fits that employee. By knowing how to talk to different types of people, the well-balanced supervisor is able to maintain all employees on the same level playing field. A good example of the well-balanced supervisor comes from a story that I was once told by one of my mentors years ago; he called it the swan theory. I have since heard this theory explained in many different venues throughout the years, it went like this. When you are managing efficiently, it is as a swan looks on the water. The swan swims so gracefully, all you see is the beautiful ebb and flow on the water's surface; however, if you were to look up underneath the water, the swan's feet and legs are kicking so hard and so fast, you cannot believe that they can be so graceful above. The well-balanced supervisor has the respect of his or her employees and is able to manage in such a way that he or she looks just like a swan on top of the water. The well-balanced supervisor is the hardest management style to maintain, but in the end, it is the best management style to have.

"The wet noodle supervisor"

The wet noodle supervisor is just as the name implies. The employees generally run the show with this type of leader. The wet noodle supervisor has the ability to complete all the tasks that are assigned to him or her, but when it comes to making sound decisions, they will only do so if they absolutely have to. Most employees love wet noodle supervisors because they feel they can do whatever they please, and that they can have things exactly the way they want them. Unfortunately, the way employees want things is not always in the best interest of the company. Wet noodle supervisors have issues with speaking to employees and to customers. The wet Noodle supervisor will often look the other way, even when it comes to issues that should require discipline. The wet noodle supervisor lacks confidence.

Earlier in this book, I pointed out that you should always try to accommodate your employee's wants and needs, but you must also be responsible in your position as a leader. If you are not being affective as a leader, the company may replace you. You are part of the company's foundation and they expect you to do a good job on all fronts. Whatever you do, do not go hard the other way and become a "big chip supervisor." Give your employees leeway, but do not jeopardize your role in the company by being led or by hiding when issues that require leadership arise. In these situations, be a leader. You should sit down and think about what type of leader you are and attempt to make changes in the areas that make you a "big chip" or a "wet noodle" type of supervisor. Listen to your employees. Listening could get you a long way in the earned respect column. Do whatever you can to help your employees succeed. Help your employees to be comfortable and satisfied with their jobs. This does not mean that you have to hold their hand or baby them. Try to encourage your employees to excel and let them know that you are behind them. Try your best to be a "well-balanced" kind of supervisor. I have had much success with this type of leadership style.

CHAPTER 6:

ORGANIZATIONAL STRESS

There are different kinds of stressors that employees will face in the workplace. If you add the stress of home life, you can double that stress. If you are an emergency person like a paramedic, police officer, firefighter, nurse, etc., you can triple the stress. As a leader for any type of organization, you must keep in mind that your employees have outside lives that may cause an enormous stress load on them. Because of this reason, you should try to keep organizational stress (stress at the workplace) at a minimum. Organizational stress can come from upper management, a low-level supervisor, and co-workers. I define normal organizational stress as the stress that an employee feels while he or she is performing the duties and tasks that are assigned to them while they are at the workplace. You may say that normal organizational stress comes with the territory and I would have to agree, general job commitments do cause a level of stress; however, what you need to avoid as a leader is exerting undue additional stress. You can avoid adding additional stress by allowing an employee to be human. Let's recall the chapter on discipline. In the discipline chapter, we discussed allowing the employee to learn from their mistakes. Do not be ready to pounce on the employee because you like to hand out discipline. If an employee feels like they are walking on eggshells and they are in fear of discipline, they will most likely make more mistakes, and this adds to organizational stress.

I will use what I call the "widget theory" to explain an example of organizational stress that was added to the workplace by a fictitious management team. For those of you who do not remember the widget, it was a small blade used for scraping stickers off windows and as a cutting tool. Here is my fictitious example. I am currently producing three-thousand widgets a day, but I am only required to make two-thousand-nine-hundred widgets a day, so I am doing great. You are my supervisor and you feel that I am not making the widgets correctly; for whatever reason, you are not satisfied with the widgets that I am turning out. You call me into your office and you give

me the news. You tell me how my widgets
are just not up to par. I explain that
the widgets are being produced as per
the exact specifications required by our
widget making manual and I ask you what is
wrong with my widgets. You explain that you
want the widgets manufactured a different
way. You want the flange for the cover of
the blade to be wider. Recently, another
supervisor on the same shift told me that
the widgets are just fine, so what do I do
now? Do I tell the supervisor who wants me
to change the way I am producing the widgets
that another supervisor told me that the
widgets are as per company specifications?
On the other hand, do I change the way I
am making the widgets? If I manufacture
the widgets the way this supervisor wants
them done, will I be out of compliance
with the company's manual? Just writing
this gives me stress. Here is what you need
to do if the employee is not making the
widgets the way they actually should be
made. This may seem obvious, but you should
show the employee how to make the widgets
properly. If the employee is already making
the widgets to specification, you need a
better reason for making a change than, "I
want the widgets made differently." This
is very important for you as a leader to
understand, especially if the employee
is producing the product as specified per

your company guidelines. The correct way to approach changing the production of the widget is for you to meet with your manager and to explain your concerns to him or her. You should tell your boss that you think the product specifications need to be changed. If your boss wants to make a change, they should take that concern to the designers and specification writers and suggest a change. If the specifications for the widget are changed, all the employees should then be re-trained to start following the new product specifications. The organizational stress that I point out in this example should be very easy to see. The employee was put in a position to feel confused and possibly very conflicted with the order from their immediate supervisor. You should try to avoid any or all issues of this nature. Another example of how organizational stress can be added to the workplace is stress caused by another employee, or by the employees themselves. Some employees will do what is barely required of them and others will be overachievers. If you place these two types of employees together, you may already guess what the problem will be. One employee is doing all kinds of work and is proud of what they accomplish. The other employee wants to coast. I am not saying that either position is wrong, as long as both employees are doing their jobs. The issue here is that sometimes an overachieving or very motivated employee will on occasion attempt to push an employee who is doing the minimum to do more. The overachiever may make comments or attempt to train the other employee, even though it is not their place to do so. This behavior can infuriate the other employee. The overachiever points out things that they feel the other employees are not doing correctly. Employees should not have to fear that other employees could get them in trouble, especially if they are doing their jobs as expected.

My last example of added organizational stress is like the overachiever, but is called the perfectionist. These people must have everything in a certain place at all times. These people tend to overanalyze and can stress everyone out because of their quirky ways. When this type of employee has free rein, they will overshadow everyone. They will move things around and change things to fit how they feel is the perfect way to have them. The stress that this type of person can cause on others is tremendous. One should not force your obsessive-compulsive disorder onto other people. My recommendation for this type of employee is to first, keep them because of their outstanding production and good work, but you may need to place them in a shop or area with other people just like them. You should give them their own work area that is separate from other types of employees. Just make sure that by separating them, it does not appear as if you are discriminating against them. If you do not choose the separation option, you should speak with the compulsive employee and steer them away from making comments to other employees. You should tell them to report directly to you if they truly feel that they have an issue that needs to be addressed.

The ultimate example of organizational stress is when an employee shows up with a gun. When this happens, it is too late to fix. When someone is pushed over the brink from being passed over for promotion, or from being discriminated against, or from having a feeling of rejection, or they feel put off in some way; the unthinkable can happen. Look at the news, employee suicide and workplace violence is becoming an epidemic.

My final words of wisdom for organizational stress are, no matter what type of business you have, let your employees be in charge of their work. If you think there is an employee performance issue, you can discuss that issue with the employee and take suitable action. Do not yell at an employee or immediately discipline them.

Talk to your employees and train them, give them the time and space they will need to improve. Put people that tend to work well together into the same groups. Make everyone as comfortable as possible as long as the job is being done. Do not make employees feel like they are walking on eggshells. The more organizational stress there is, the worse the product, or the worse the service that is provided will be. Examine your workplace and find out how you can reduce organizational stress, do not wait until it is too late.

CHAPTER 7:

A HAPPIER WORKPLACE

To this point, my book has been primarily focused on what not to do as a leader. This chapter discusses some of the things that you should do to ensure stability among the employees in your workplace. There is no way I can explain every possible way for you to contribute to a happy workplace. What I can do is give you a few examples of things that were very successful for me. Use these examples if you think they might work for you. The first thing you should do to change things for the good is to give your employees a voice. Allowing your employees to have a voice in the company will make them feel like management cares about their ideas enough to let them be a part of the organization's decision-making processes. Great ideas were born from people on the frontlines of many businesses. The employees are the ones who are using the manufacturing equipment daily and they are the ones delivering the services to the customer. The employees know many things about the business and the products. If only one employee changes a design that builds a better mousetrap, you could prosper. If several employees get together to discuss how to improve the effectiveness of an assembly line or to discuss how to build a better product and they succeed, how can you lose? It is very simple, just listen.

Another way to help make a happier workplace is to reward your employees for their great work. This is a low cost, big payback item. A certificate that says "thank you" can be produced on your computer. Just make sure that you place the certificate in a nice frame. You can create a certificate for, a job well done, a high level of production, attendance, and whatever else you can think of; recognition goes a long way. Having an employee of the month and employee of the year also feeds employee morale. I want to point out that you should not pick a person for employee of the month or employee of the year because it is their turn. Make guidelines and have employees and supervisors nominate the deserving person based on attitude, success, and job performance. Company picnics and Christmas parties can also go a long way. I understand that parties can cost some money, so I suggest that you budget for these things in advance. I used to give out prizes like flashlights and firefighter tools that my employees could use on the job. These ideas are just suggestions because they worked for me. Ultimately, you should tailor your employee recognition program to your workplace.

Something that was very easy to do and had good payback in promoting a positive workplace was providing my employees with surveys. The survey asked the employees outright; "Hi, how are you doing out there? Is there anything that I can do in order to improve your working environment?" A very simple five-question survey works. Make sure that you do not ask for the employee's name or other identifying information, some employees are very skittish and think if they say anything, they may get in trouble.

Another example I have seen help to improve employee morale is allowing employees to attend workshops and meetings. I would encourage my employees to participate in educational opportunities and other planning meetings. Allowing an employee to attend these meetings makes them feel ownership in the organization. Not all employees will respond to this, but there is a huge psychological affect on the employee when you encourage them to be a part of the organization. One note of caution however, do not shake your head and take notes and say, "Oh yeah thank you for that idea" and then never use the idea. This behavior eventually gets old and the employees stop attending meetings because they know that inviting them is just a snow job. To simplify what I just said, if you do not care about your employee's ideas, do not invite them to the meetings. Inviting your employees to meetings and blowing off their idea is much worse than not inviting them to a meeting at all. If you feel that one of your employee's ideas will not work, discuss the reasons why at the meeting. Get feedback from all of the attendees. If you receive feedback that backs up your decision, you can then let everyone know that this information supports why you will not use the idea. After the feedback session, you may decide that the idea is actually a workable one. By using this technique it allows the employee who came up with the idea and all the other employees to fully understand why you are, or why you are not using the idea. This technique really helps to prevent dissention within the company.

One last example of what I liked when I was an employee was having clean working facilities. Having a clean kitchen to make my lunch in, and having a clean bathroom to do my business in was very important to me. Having a refrigerator and a water cooler were also great. Consider having a nice place for your employees to take their breaks.

In actuality, this entire book is about how to make your place of business a happier workplace. The bottom line is, if you remember how you felt as an employee when you worked for someone else, or if you realize how what you do as a manager affects your employee's morale, you will be able to change the way you do things for the positive. All businesses are different and I am not saying that all of my advice in this chapter can be used, but you should sit down and consider your options, especially if you think there is a problem with employee happiness and morale. If you think that your production or customer service is lacking, you most certainly should try a few of the techniques that I mentioned, you have nothing to lose.

CHAPTER 8:

MASLOW'S HIERARCHY OF NEEDS

Until now, everything in this book has been from my own knowledge and experiences. I feel that I would be remiss if I did not offer the information that I learned from studying Mr. Abraham Maslow. Mr. Maslow was a psychologist that developed a theory outlining motivational factors of people. I have read about this theory in several books and I have observed how this theory works first hand. Although some psychologists still call Maslow's theory un-proven, I believe that Maslow's theory makes sense; you can decide for yourself. *Maslow says that humans are motivated by need; he developed what is known today as "Maslow's Hierarchy of Needs." These needs are said to be progressive in nature and are depicted in the scheme of a pyramid. At the bottom of the pyramid are the basic physiological needs. Physiological needs are food, water, clothing, and shelter. Most people obtain basic needs by working a job and by receiving a paycheck. With a job and a steady income, you can maintain your basic needs by purchasing them. As explained in the theory, humans will not move to the next level until all basic needs are met. The next level in Maslow's Hierarchy of needs is "safety and security." Safety and security will consist of maintaining wealth through insurance policies, bank accounts, and other benefits that may be provided by an employer. In my own opinion, this is like having an insurance policy to protect your basic accumulation in case you were to lose your job or be unable to work. This level is closely related to basic physiological need. The next level in Maslow's Hierarchy is "social need." This need equates to belonging to a group, or being part of some kind of social activity. Some examples of social activities or groups are, The Boy Scouts of America, Brownie Troops, a playing card club, or shooting pool on Wednesday nights with friends.The next level in Maslow's theory is "esteem and status." The esteem and status need involves ego-fulfillment. People will attempt to achieve esteem and status through recognition at work or recognition in a group. Receiving a promotion or a certificate of honor make people feel recognized, self-respect is a part of this level. At the top of Maslow's pyramid is self-actualization and fulfillment. When you reach this stage, it means that you have accomplished a goal. It means that you are in a time and place where you have succeeded at some rewarding thing in your life. For example, you could have just made CEO of a company or Lieutenant at the fire department. When you reach self-actualization, you may find a need to attain a different goal. People will run up and down the pyramid as needed throughout their lives. The one thing that I noticed is that when I reached the top of the pyramid, I looked for another goal. When I became a District Fire Chief, it took me about five years in that position before I wanted to be a Fire Chief for an entire department. Since all my other needs were met, I spent several years attempting to reach my new goal, which I eventually did; I became the Fire Chief of a department.

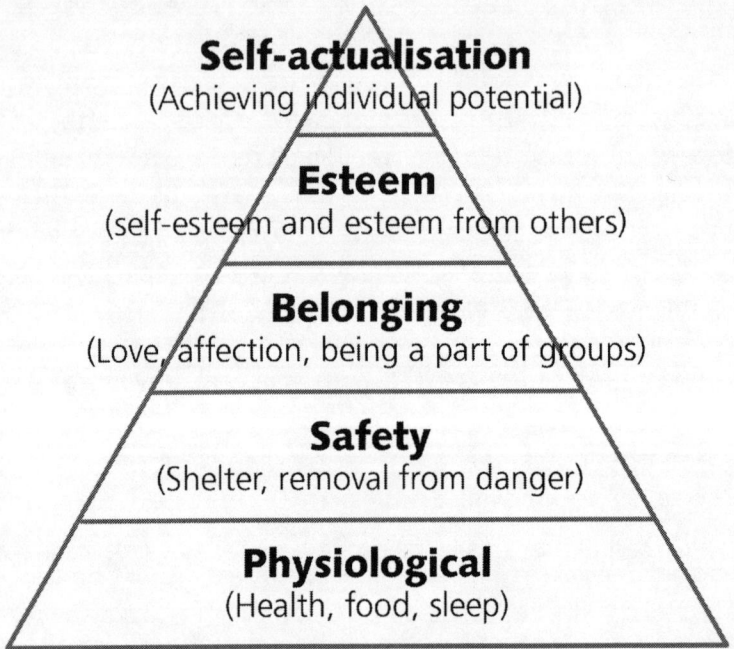

An example of Maslow's conceptualization
of the levels of basic human needs.

*"Management in the Fire Service"
Harry R. Carter and Erwin Rausch
National Fire Protection Agency
Second addition

CHAPTER 9:

EVALUATIONS

I want to discuss how employee evaluations can be used to make a better and more productive workplace for both the employer and the employee. There are two types of evaluations that I will discuss. One evaluation is the yearly or annual evaluation and the other evaluation is the pre-evaluation. The pre-evaluation is just as it sounds, it is an evaluation that does not count towards the employee's performance or his or her raise; it lets the employee know where they stand and how they can improve long before they receive their actual evaluation. Not all organizations use a pre-evaluation and I often wondered why. In doing some research, I found that many leaders simply did not think of using a pre-evaluation, or they had never heard of a pre-evaluation program. I am a huge proponent of the pre-evaluation.

The pre-evaluation:

Before you do an anniversary date evaluation for an employee, you give them what I call, "a state of their performance evaluation" or pre-evaluation. This evaluation can be in the form of a letter, or in the form of a conversation between you and the employee. The pre-evaluation is what you can use to advise the employee about what areas they are not excelling in, or where you see they can use improvement with their job performance. The pre-evaluation works great for a few reasons. One reason I found is that the employee sees that you care about their success by sharing this information with them. Instead of slamming them at their annual or bi-annual evaluation, you give them a heads up. Many leaders do not care enough to provide this information to their employees, some leaders love to hurt people by giving out a poor evaluation; they get off on it. Every time I used the pre-evaluation, I turned out employees who excelled in their positions. The employees in my case were firefighters. After I spent a year helping a firefighter by showing them what they were weak in, they would feel bad if they did not perform well for me. I know this because I had a few employees start to slack a little and tell me that they were not putting in one-hundred-percent. They let me know that it was not for my lack of training; just that they were taking a small break or that they were getting lazy. I always told them that I understood because I have been there myself; being a new employee is hard in any job. If an employee knows that you care, I promise that they will do a better job because of the time you took to provide them with the tools that they needed to succeed and because they respect you.

I suggest that you conduct a monthly pre-evaluation. Providing a pre-evaluation on a monthly bases does two things. It gives you time to collect data on the performance of the employee, and it gives the employee eleven pre-evaluations before they get an annual evaluation. Some companies will give a six-month evaluation so that an employee can take advantage of a raise at six months. If this is what your company does, it is still ok to do a monthly pre-evaluation. The evaluation should be simple, but it should have enough information to inform the employee on what you see as needing improvement. With that said, I would not create a pre-evaluation that is more than two pages in length. Some of the questions I asked on my pre-evaluation dealt with employee timeliness. Does the employee arrive to work on time and does the employee finish their work in a timely manner? Other questions I had on my pre-evaluation dealt with safety, attitude towards the public, professionalism, cleanliness, and work ethic. Many of these questions are meant to be objective instead of subjective. This may be hard to understand because you can be subjective on all of these if you want. The way to take out the subjectivity is to have written rules that outline exactly what each example means. In short, cleanliness may state that the employee is clean-shaven and appears groomed. This is easy to see when the employee comes to work. I can go on forever with examples, you need to see what your company requirements are for each position that you are evaluating and go from there. Whatever you choose, keep the documentation so you can go back and review what you talked to the employee about. It is not a bad idea to have the employee sign the pre-evaluation form, but you may have to answer to a union. Union leaders do not like employees to sign anything that may get them in some kind of trouble. Even though the pre-evaluation is to help the employee, there may be a perception from some folks that it is not. Most evaluations including the pre-evaluation are probably covered under management rights if you do work in a union shop. The Human Resources Director is an excellent source of information to make sure you are keeping things in the green so to speak.

The Annual evaluation:

The annual evaluation is used to advise an employee about how he or she is performing after one year of performance in the workplace. The annual evaluation can also be used to determine how much of a raise to give the employee, or to allow the employee to get off of a probationary status. Some organizations will also reference past annual evaluations if an employee is up for a promotion. By looking back at annual evaluations, the leadership can get a snap shot of how the employee has been performing.

The annual or semi-annual evaluation is mainly used to help direct and improve an employee's work performance; it is a report card. I had an employee that was a little sluggish when it came to fire department station duties like station clean up, answering the phone, and other housekeeping duties. At evaluation time, I brought the employee into my office and we discussed the different areas of the evaluation where I felt he was lacking. I scored the employee mediocre in every category that fit his need for improvement; however, I could have scored him lower in these categories solely based on his poor performance. I explained to the employee that I felt he scored lower than I had ranked him and that I scored him mediocre because I was sure he could improve and I wanted to give him a chance to do so. To other managers, the way I handled this employee evaluation could have been viewed as if I was not doing my job, but the outcome was that the employee excelled in all the areas that I had discussed with him. Let me explain why this happened. The employee respected the fact that I told him about his shortcomings and that I did not nail him on the evaluation for the big bosses to see. In turn, the employee improved and is now one of the best firefighters I have. The employee fed off the fact that I gave him a break, that I took the time to explain what he was not accomplishing rather than filling out a poor evaluation. As I stated earlier in the pre-evaluation section, many supervisors get enjoyment out of tendering poor evaluations even if they are not warranted, this is a bad idea; do not forward a bad evaluation unless you have to.

Another firefighter who had just started with me was a poor out of the gate performer. I believe it was because he was twenty-three and had never been part of an organization such as the fire service. The fire service is big on having the lowest peg on the totem pole do most of the grunt work. Grunt work usually consists of doing the dishes, answering the phone, cleaning the toilets and all the stuff you would expect a probationary firefighter to do. Anyway, this firefighter would sleep through our normal wake-up time while everyone else started the morning station clean up at seven. Here is what I did. I asked the firefighter to meet me in the back of the fire station, not in my office. I did this to avoid embarrassment. I spoke with the employee about him not getting up at our normal wake-up time. I explained that his performance was not acceptable and that he needed to start the day with everyone else. I also told him that I understand what it is like to be up all night running calls and then to have to get up first thing in the morning. The firefighter told me that he understood and that he was sorry. My first thought was, we shall see. Unfortunately, the firefighter again slept through the morning details. Now mind you, there were much more senior firefighters including myself, doing the morning chores while this guy slept, so you can see how this did not go over well. This kind of situation is why monthly evaluations or pre-evaluations for the first year are good for probationary employees; it tells them how they are doing. The next shift, I explained to the employee that I did not want to mark him low in the "completes all work assigned category", but that he was leaving me no choice. I asked him if he would keep an eye on this situation for me, this was my last warning. To my amazement, the firefighter continued to get up late. It was very simple for me at this point. On the next evaluation, I marked the firefighter as "needs improvement" and sent the paperwork into headquarters. That evaluation became part of his permanent record. I continued to be this firefighter's supervisor, so I gave him more tips on how to get up on time. I told him to make sure that he has an alarm clock. I told him to have one of the other firefighters wake him up. After we reviewed his official evaluation, he apologized for not complying with my directions. I told him that at this point it is up to him. I am no longer concerned with sending in a low score because I did my best to help him to succeed. I explained to the firefighter that because we had already spoken several times about this situation there were no more chances. I was now in a position to move towards discipline if the employee did not follow through the next shift and he knew this. The next shift, the employee showed up with a brand new alarm clock, a smile on his face and he never got up late again. This is a true story. The employee's next evaluation showed his improvement and to this day, he gets up on time. I know that it looks like I gave this guy too many chances, but this is a different style of management, one you will have to get used to. In the end, you will reap the benefits. You really earn points giving your employees some room here, but as everything else, this is not 100% foolproof. You need to know that you will get the occasional employee who will take advantage of this leadership style and will take you all the way through the first tier of discipline before they actually show improvement. Some employees will end up terminated because they just don't get it, but at least you know that you gave them plenty of chances to succeed and allowed them plenty of room for improvement.

CHAPTER 10:

PAT'S THEORY ON QUALITY MANAGEMENT

Total Quality Management (TQM) techniques can be applied to many different industries and organizations. I have mainly used (TQM) in the medical care industry. When applying the knowledge of total quality management, it is very important that you and your employees understand that quality management is meant to be non-punitive. There should never be discipline issued from a situation that is being evaluated for improvement as long as improvement is being made. Without the fear of discipline, you have more employee buy-in and involvement with the program. Your employees should understand that the re-training that you provide is to help them to do their jobs better.

Whatever you want to call it, quality improvement, total quality management, or quality assurance, (I use these terms interchangeably) it is a way to improve employee performance. The very first step before starting any type of (TQM) program is to explain the entire program to all of your employees. You need to set up a training class and before that class, you should have all your tools ready. By tools I mean you should have a printed manual that states how the program will work and how you expect to deliver feedback to the employees. An easy to read manual will allow the employee to self-train to a point and will allow the employee to have reference material for things they will forget as time goes on. Some other tools that you will need are examples of each product or service that your organization provides. You must show the employees the exact way you want them to sell or to produce the product, these methods should be introduced in a classroom atmosphere. Another very important aspect of maintaining a (TQM) program is to make sure that you keep records with good documentation of all the training sessions that take place. You may wish to consider what I call a training verification form (TVF). A training verification form is a form that shall include the date, time, place, and type of training that was provided to the employee. All the employees who were involved in the training will sign the form and you will file the form in a quality assurance folder that is separate from all of the other employee records. You can also use a standard roster of attendance as long as your roster lists the date, time, place and the training that took place for that session. You can recall the quality assurance folder when and if it is needed to talk to an employee about their on-going performance. When re-trained, an employee should never feel like they are being made an example of, nor should they feel embarrassed about requiring additional training. If you find that you do have an employee or employees that are not cutting the mustard, you need to take the employee into a classroom setting and provide additional training. In this type of remedial session, you start by explaining the issues that you are finding with the product or service delivery. You discuss how the organization plans to help the employee to improve through the (QA) program. Provide additional education to your employees about different ways of getting to the end goal, the goal of producing a good product or delivering a good service. Make all your quality management meetings enjoyable; make the employees part of the improvement team. Do not forget to praise the good things that your employees have been doing. When you are finished with a remedial training session, put your employees back to work, hopefully with a new and positive outlook. Over the next several months, see if the products or service delivery has improved. In most cases there will be mild to moderate improvement. In some cases, the problem will be completely fixed and you may not have to speak to that employee or group of employees again. The idea is to speak with the employees having the most problems only a few times. You can simply monitor the progress and flag any issues from there.

Ok, it gets a little sticky here. Earlier in this chapter I explain that the total quality management process should not be punitive; however, if an employee is not improving after three to five sessions of re-training, it is time to consider the value of that employee. What is that employee costing the company in customers or product wastage? If you find that an employee is not working out, you have to take that employee aside and explain to them that they are not performing as well as you had hoped; this is even after all the training that you provided. At this point, you will explain to the employee that they will be removed from the quality management program and that further errors may lead to progressive discipline. It is here that the employee will either make or break their career. If the employee continues to decline, they will eventually be released from the organization. It is for this reason that you need to keep good records. When you have an appropriate file that shows all of the training that the organization has provided, you have legally moved in a direction that will most likely keep you out of legal hot water once you go over the file with the employee.

I have only scratched the surface of dealing with the success of how a good quality management program should be instituted. Make sure that you educate your employees about why you are starting the quality assurance program. Make sure that you keep good records and try to get everyone involved. Total quality management is not an alternative to the disciplinary process. The goal of total quality management (TQM) is to ensure that your team will turn out a good product and deliver a good service. The direction of (TQM) should always be to drive incremental improvement so that the company can appreciate increased profits and happy customers. Use quality management tools and techniques to become an educational leader.

CHAPTER 11:

WRAP UP

Many things happened to me since I started writing this book. I got married, I had a child, and I was promoted to District Fire Chief. These things did not necessarily happen in that exact order. As I moved forward with my career, I found myself needing to add more and more to this book, but I know that I needed to stop somewhere, because I want to get this information out to you. The techniques that I mention in this book have worked countless times in my career. Remember, this is a simple approach. Other books dig much deeper into the human psyche and will have all kinds of studies that will teach you about management. Personally, I do not believe that the art of managing people as a science will ever change because humans tend to remain static in the working arena. What I mean is, there are different personalities and if you apply what you know to each personality, you will be able to figure out how to work with each employee. Do not be discouraged if you change your management style and there is no affect over night. It may take time to take a dog that has been beaten for years and make him or her realize that it is okay to come out of the corner. You need to give the dog time to see that it is ok to run across the yard. Another point to consider is that you will not make all of your employees happy, but I guarantee you have the ability to grant employee wishes and to show your employees that you care. This one change will pay you back in large dividends. Allow your employees to feel like they are a part of the organization instead of telling them to show up, do not be late, and work your tail off. Find ways to decrease organizational stress and to increase employee loyalty; employee morale directly increases production. Pride in work performance and the outcome of the finished product has a lot to do with how an employee feels about the work they do. If I were to hire a ship building company to build a seventy-five foot sailboat, I would hope that the people building the boat would build it correctly. It would not be savory if when I was thirty miles off shore, the boat started to sink. If the employees of the boat building company are total quality and excellence of craft minded and they are praised for the outstanding work that they turn out, most employees will continue to produce a great product. If employees feel that they are unfairly treated, poorly paid, or that they lack other job amenities, they will do a halfhearted job. The last thing you want is for employees to work slower, call out sick more, and cost the company money. My point throughout this entire book has been to treat your employees well, but within your means. You have to quell the "big chip" supervisors and make sure that you and your staff are fair and consistent at all times. Have good working conditions and do not skimp on praise when it is due. You will not make every employee happy, but all you need to do is have the majority of the employees happy; the rest will follow, leave, or fire them-selves. If you continue to say no to everything that your employees ask for, you will bring the company's production and employee satisfaction down. Listen to this advice, I have seen a lack of morale destroy a group of workers and put them at each other's throats.

Here are a few other things for you to do. Get out there on the floor and work with your employees, get to know them and find out what makes them tick. Many leaders will not do this because it is hard work and it is time consuming, but I promise you it is the right thing to do. Your employees will see your presence as positive as long as you are not out there beating them over the head. If you are out there to help them and to talk with them, you will gain respect. I also want you to remember the following. The worst thing you can do is to lie, cheat, or steal from your employees. If your employees feel that you are not genuine, they will clam up and you will lose trust. If you lose trust, it takes forever to get the trust back, if you can even earn the trust a second time. Be real and be genuine; take care of your people. If after you read this book you feel like these techniques are asking you to reduce your power as a leader, or if you feel like you would not want to try to be anything other than a heavy-fisted micromanaging person, then you will see problems in your leadership future.